WHO TOLD YOU YOU'RE IN A SEASON OF WAITING?

ALSO FROM REVIVAL TODAY

Financial Overflow

Dominion Over Sickness and Disease

Boldly I Come

Twenty Secrets for an Unbreakable Marriage

How to Dominate in a Wicked Nation

Seven Wrong Relationships

Everything a Man Should Be

Understanding the World in Light of Bible Prophecy

Are You Going Through a Crisis?

The 20 Laws that Govern the Financial Anointing

35 Questions for Those Who Hate the Prosperity Gospel

The Art of Spiritual Warfare

Help for Your Darkest Time

Seven Reasons Your Church Will Never Have Revival

Who Told You You're in a Season of Waiting?

How to Prevail in Every Battle of Life

Decisions Determine Destiny

Twenty-Four Changes to Immediately Improve Your Happiness

Taking Your Place at the Top

The Path to Dominion: A 16-Week Devotional to Walk in God's Plan for Your Life

WHO TOLD YOU YOU'RE IN A SEASON OF WAITING?

6 DESTINY CHANGING DECISIONS YOU CAN MAKE TODAY

JONATHAN SHUTTLESWORTH

Without limiting the rights under copyright(s) reserved below, no part of this publication may be reproduced, stored in, or introduced into a retrieval system, or transmitted in any form or by any means (electronic, mechanical, photocopying, recording, or otherwise) without the prior permission of the publisher and the copyright owner.

The content of this book is provided "AS IS." The publisher and the author make no guarantees or warranties as to the accuracy, adequacy, or completeness of or results to be obtained from using the content of this book, including any information that can be accessed through hyperlinks or otherwise, and expressly disclaim any warranty expressed or implied, including but not limited to implied warranties of merchantability or fitness for a particular purpose. This limitation of liability shall apply to any claim or cause whatsoever, whether such claim or cause arises in contract, tort, or otherwise. In short, you, the reader, are responsible for your choices and the results they bring.

The scanning, uploading, and distributing of this book via the internet or any other means without the permission of the publisher and copyright owner is illegal and punishable by law. Please purchase only authorized copies, and do not participate in or encourage piracy of copyrighted materials. Your support of the author's rights is appreciated.

Unless otherwise marked, Scriptures are taken from the HOLY BIBLE, NEW LIVING TRANSLATION (NLT): Scriptures taken from the HOLY BIBLE, NEW LIVING TRANSLATION, Copyright© 1996, 2004, 2007 by Tyndale House Foundation. Used by permission of Tyndale House Publishers, Inc., Carol Stream, Illinois 60188. All rights reserved. Used by permission.

Scriptures marked KJV are taken from the KING JAMES VERSION (KJV): KING JAMES VERSION, public domain.

Copyright © 2024 by Revival Today. All rights reserved.

Released: November 2024
Updated: August 2025
ISBN: 978-1-64457-726-4

Rise UP Publications
www.riseUPpublications.com
Phone: 866-846-5123

For God is working in you, giving you the desire and the power to do what pleases him.

— PHILIPPIANS 2:13

CONTENTS

Preface — 9
Introduction — 15

Part I
DESTINY-CHANGING PRINCIPLES

Chapter 1 — 21
Success is a Product of Action

Chapter 2 — 29
Seasons of Waiting Are Not Scriptural

Chapter 3 — 35
Decisions Create Seasons

Part II
DESTINY-CHANGING DECISIONS

Chapter 4 — 47
Don't Allow What You Don't Desire

Chapter 5 — 49
Do What Satan Hates

Chapter 6 — 53
Determine to Bear Fruit in Every Season

Chapter 7 — 59
Refuse to Quit

Chapter 8 — 65
Find Your Place

Chapter 9 — 67
Begin Today

Part III
DESTINY-CHANGING ACTIONS

Chapter 10 — 71
Avoid Zeal Killers

Chapter 11 — 73
Seek Accomplished Counselors

Chapter 12 — 75
Praise

Chapter 13	77
Enact the Power of Prayer and Fasting	
Chapter 14	79
Change Your Confession	
Chapter 15	81
Run with Runners – Don't Sit with Sitters	
Chapter 16	83
Encounter Jesus	
Afterword	85
Author Photo	88
About the Author	90

PREFACE

The Devil will try to get you to attribute your lack of productivity to a season of waiting. When you believe your life is subject to God-ordained dry seasons and that your productivity is solely orchestrated by a sovereign God who pulls your strings, you become immobilized and powerless. It's hard to imagine a belief more aligned with the Devil's desires than this.

 There is no gift of waiting for miracles. There is a gift of the working of miracles.

Jesus took spit and put it in the mute man's mouth, and the man spoke. Actions elicit miracles. Reinhard Bonnke used to say, "God goes with the goers. He doesn't sit with the sitters." Are you unhappy with your life? Are there elements of your life you're unsatisfied with? Are you quietly and patiently waiting for things to change? If you are, it's probably not your fault. You're aligned with the majority of preaching you hear. Few ministers preach that your decisions determine your destiny. I'm not claiming I'm better than other ministers, but what I'm going to cover isn't preached very often.

People teach that life is a waiting game: "We don't know why things are happening the way they are, but we just have to trust God during this season of sickness." No, exit the season by making a decision. Decide to act on what the Bible says.

> Are any among you sick? They should call on the elders of the church, anoint them with oil, and their prayer offered in faith will save the sick and the Lord will raise them up. And any sins they've committed will be forgiven.
>
> — JAMES 5:14-15

In this scripture, the sick person is the one who is called upon to act. The woman with the issue of blood changed her season of infirmity through her actions. It wasn't God's decision; it was her decision. She made up her mind. She said to herself, 'I know if I touch the hem of His garment, I will be made well.' She decided to snap herself out of her stale, stagnant, and unproductive season. You can decide to do the same thing by saying, "I'm not waiting. I'm coming out today."

I've met Christians in their 60s and 70s who have said, "When I was younger, I had someone prophesy that I would see a stadium filled and that many people would be saved. I just know that word is going to come to pass." Sadly, it won't.

Before we held Steel City Fest in Pittsburgh, Pastor Rodney Howard-Browne prophesied, "I see a stadium being filled and people coming down from the stands onto the field to receive Christ." He told me privately, "It'll be a smaller field and then a bigger one in the future."

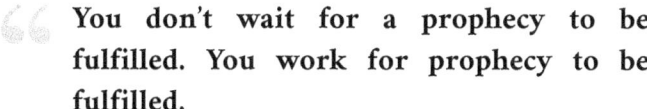

You don't wait for a prophecy to be fulfilled. You work for prophecy to be fulfilled.

You have most likely received a word from the Lord in some area of your life. But you have to ask further questions like:

> *"What actions must I take to cause this to bear fruit?"*
> *"Now that I've heard the Word of the Lord, what position do I take to make it happen?"*
> *"Where do I go?"*
> *"What do I need to acquire?"*

Someone might claim, "I received a word that I would be an influential government leader who helps turn the nation's heart back to God." Okay, great. What are you doing to see that fulfilled?

Another person might say, "I'm just in a dry financial season. I lost my job, and I know the Lord will give me a better one." Yes, but you need to go where the jobs are. Do

PREFACE

you think a CEO will show up in your living room? Your decisions can snap you out of a dry season.

When I graduated from Bible College on May 10, 2002, I was off to the races. People told me things like, "You're too young to start traveling. Who wants to hear what a 21-year-old has to say for a week straight?" My response was, "I don't know, but I'll find somebody because I'm doing this. I'm going to run. I'm not going to assume an inferior posture. I won't wait to age into my calling."

 Until you make different decisions, nothing changes.

If you're in your twenties, do you think everything will magically fall into place when you reach thirty? I hit a breakthrough at thirty years old, but I hit it running. I wasn't waiting back then, and I'm not waiting now. Nothing will change ten years from now unless I continue to run.

The Bible says, *"Life is but a vapor. Here today, gone tomorrow"* (James 4:14). Life has brevity. I believe in God's promise of a long life, but a long life is relative. Ninety years go by quickly. I'm almost halfway to ninety right now and feel like I've just started. The first forty-three years went fast. You genuinely can't afford to let a month go by, let alone years, without moving forward. You only get a few years on this earth. You must run in a forward direction each day.

Many people struggle to discover their purpose. Until you figure out what your purpose is, find someone who knows theirs and work alongside them—lessons from the life of Lot. Lot had no encounters with God, but Abraham did. So, he hitched his wagon to him, and he went forward. That may be your purpose. There's nothing wrong with being Billy Graham's crusade director. He made a huge impact. But don't wait to connect with someone who's moving forward, do it now.

There was a time when we had a dozen or so full-time staff in our ministry, and now we employ over fifty full-time employees. Some people moved here, showed up, and started volunteering. They stood out, so we hired them full-time. I take it seriously when someone is willing to leave everything behind and move for something they're passionate about. Serious people don't wait for change, they enforce it. Who told you you're in a season of waiting? It certainly wasn't God.

INTRODUCTION

PROPHECY SHOULD PROVOKE ACTION

> But Moses told the people, "Don't be afraid. Just stand still and watch the Lord rescue you today. The Egyptians you see today will never be seen again. The Lord himself will fight for you. Just stay calm."
>
> — EXODUS 14:13-14

Moses was later rebuked for what he told the Israelites. People who never amount to anything have two traits in common: they stand still, and they watch.

> Then the Lord said to Moses, "Why are you crying out to me? Tell the people to get moving!"
>
> — EXODUS 14:15

The Israelites prayed when God had already told them to act, and it irritated Him. *"Why are you crying out to me?"*

INTRODUCTION

God gave Moses a rod and told him to use it to perform signs and wonders. God told him He would make him as a God to Pharoah. Moses attempted to back out of his God-given assignment. Many ministers are still doing the same thing today. They may disguise it as some religious exercise in patience or prayer, but it's an excuse for inaction. Some things should be prayed about, and others should not be prayed about—they should be acted upon.

I was raised in a Pentecostal church. Pentecostals are the kings and queens of waiting. "Oh Lord, send revival. We're waiting on You, oh Lord, to move Thy hand through this nation." Meanwhile, God is in Heaven trying to figure out what Bible they're reading. He's done. He sent His Son. Jesus redeemed us, then He sent the Holy Spirit and gave us all power and dominion over the Devil. There's nothing else for Him to do. Those same Pentecostal churches are still in their moldy buildings with musty, smelly carpeting, believing God will send revival. I had to snap out of that mindset. I'm glad I didn't sit back and say, "Brother Rodney once came to our church and said we're going to fill a stadium. Praise God, I know one day that time will come."

How would Steel City Fest have come to pass if I was content to sit in my office and pray? When you believe the word given to you, you do what it requires. When I received this word, I began to think about what I needed to set my faith for and what I needed to do. I began thinking of stadiums that matched the description of what Rodney saw in his vision. That notion wasn't far-fetched. It required me to secure a stadium and devise a plan to fill it with people who needed to hear the Gospel.

Once you receive a word or confirmation from the Lord or one of His servants, it's your responsibility to use your God-given brain to come up with a plan of action to make it come to pass. You'll soon discover that as you begin to act, God will lead and guide you. Half the fun of life is reasoning and meditating in your spirit about how you can bring a vision to pass with God's help, favor, and power.

 There are no dry seasons.

Even if there are natural reasons to expect a dry season, refuse to allow it in your faith. If you feed on outside information—especially negative information—there will always be ample reasons for inaction.

When the Lord told me to start a church, the price of steel tripled almost immediately. A building that could have been built for $1.6 million had increased to $5 million. It's never the wrong time to move forward in the direction God has pointed you toward. The sooner, the better. God knows what's happening on the Earth. He wasn't in Heaven stressed about the costs of building after He told me to build a church.

The Bible says, *"The Lord is not willing that any should perish, so he is giving time for people to repent and be saved"* (2 Peter 3:9). That's what God wants done. When I move forward in the direction God instructed, He will help me. The same is true for you.

Maybe you're not a pastor or an evangelist. Maybe you've connected your business to winning souls. Many business owners give substantially to our ministry. Do you think God wants you to have fewer resources or more resources? Do you believe God is too unintelligent to find a way to navigate or supernaturally overtake what's going on in the world?

The first thing you need to do if you're going to accomplish anything of value is to get rid of your love for defeat, victimhood, and fleshly desires. Don't use any incapability you may have as an excuse not to move forward. God will renew your mind and cleanse you of all unrighteousness. Don't confess your weakness or focus on your shortcomings. He will take care of what you can't do when you do what you can do. God's not concerned with your limitations, He is unlimited and He lives on the inside of you!

PART I
DESTINY-CHANGING PRINCIPLES

CHAPTER ONE

SUCCESS IS A PRODUCT OF ACTION

God has promised us prosperity and success in everything we do. Whatever you're facing today, the scriptures below address it.

> "Moses my servant is dead. Therefore, the time has come for you to lead these people, the Israelites, across the Jordan River into the land I am giving them. I promise you what I promised Moses: 'Wherever you set foot, you will be on land I have given you—from the Negev wilderness in the south to the Lebanon mountains in the north, from the Euphrates River in the east to the Mediterranean Sea in the west, including all the land of the Hittites.' No one will be able to stand against you as long as you live. For I will be with you as I was with Moses. I will not fail you or abandon you.
>
> "Be strong and courageous, for you are the one who will lead these people to possess all the

land I swore to their ancestors I would give them. Be strong and very courageous. Be careful to obey all the instructions Moses gave you. Do not deviate from them, turning either to the right or to the left. Then you will be successful in everything you do. Study this Book of Instruction continually. Meditate on it day and night so you will be sure to obey everything written in it. Only then will you prosper and succeed in all you do."

— JOSHUA 1:2-8

 You can prosper and succeed in everything you do.

What a tremendous promise that should set you at ease. Success and prosperity are in the Bible whether people like it or not. This isn't the only instance, there are similar scriptures throughout the Bible.

So why are Christians averse to prosperity, success, land ownership, and buildings? Casinos build multi-billion-dollar facilities every time you turn around. But when the conversation shifts to include Christian buildings and property acquisition, it's not too long before other Christians comment, "It's not about buildings. It's not about success." No, it actually is about those things. To those who insist, "Church isn't about buildings; church is about people." I agree, but once you get those people saved, you must disciple them. To do that, you need to gather them somewhere. If you gather people together in a field when the temperature is minus twenty degrees, you'll lose some converts when they die from exposure—buildings matter. There's a reason civilization has advanced from gathering in caves.

Don't be a bozo Christian. Don't be an idiot who always has something harsh to say about success, land, or buildings. I've heard pastors say, "We're not going to sell out the glory of God in this church so that we can have a building." You don't have to sell out to obtain a church building. The Temple in the Old Testament tells of God's glory filling a building. God is not against buildings. There are thousands of beautiful churches all over the world and they were not built by the Devil. God gave people plans to acquire the land to build them. Land ownership matters.

Part of breaking out of a "dry season" or "season of waiting" is to understand God isn't going to *give* you prosperity. God isn't going to *give* you success. You *carry* prosperity and success right now.

I went to Bible college for four years. I'm not against training, but even while in school, I wasn't in a dry season or a season of waiting. While in Bible college, a door opened for me to begin preaching in Lexington, Massachusetts. I became the youth pastor and preached on Sundays. During that time, I was given the opportunity to preach the adult service, and, in that meeting, a woman undergoing cancer treatment was healed. It wasn't until after I graduated from Bible school and began my ministry that I realized God teaches on the job.

As God continues to grow this ministry, I'm constantly reminded of times that many would consider "small beginnings," when God was preparing me to do things on a much larger scale. As I watched all those people stream down the stadium aisles and onto the field to get saved during Steel City Fest, I was reminded of something that had happened years prior. After an all-night prayer meeting, I mentioned to Adalis, "Who knew when we rented Helene Hall in Hana-Maui many years ago that this would happen today?"

Hana-Maui was the first neutral venue I'd ever rented. Before that, I had only been invited to preach in churches with members and regular attendance. The hall I rented in Hana-Maui seated about 150 people. To fill the venue, we had to invite people to attend. We brought around thirty people from the mainland. An additional twenty came on the first night for a total of about fifty people. Little did I know that was training. God knew I would soon need to secure a bigger venue and draw a hundred times that many people in the future.

God teaches you on the job. I didn't realize it at the time, but my experience in Hana-Maui was preparation for Steel City Fest. If I had never preached at a neutral venue, I would have had no idea what was required to fill one, and attempting to fill Highmark Stadium would have likely overwhelmed me.

God doesn't need to take you to the desert to train you for forty years. People who believe in a season of waiting will stay in a season of waiting for the rest of their lives. It's a demonic tactic to convince people that inaction is a spiritually beneficial concept.

The only thing separating me from all those who prophesied, "Revival is coming, and stadiums will be packed," is that I decided to act. I decided if the Lord wants revival with packed stadiums, then let's get a stadium and pack it. Let's find a way to bring the invisible Word of God into visible, tangible reality. We checked which stadiums were available. We strategized how we would fill them. Solving the problems that stand in the way becomes an adventure of life. Think, meditate, and pray. Get around wise people and find ways to realize your dream.

On April 27, 2022, Pastor Rodney Howard Browne prophesied that Revival Today would host an event at a stadium in Pittsburgh, and thousands of people would come down from the stands onto the field. We moved in the direction of the word of the Lord that was delivered through Pastor Rodney, and by Labor Day weekend of the same year, it had come to pass. I didn't sit around and talk about it for twenty years. "One day back in 2022, Pastor Rodney gave me a word that I would see a stadium filled." I want you to understand how to act in life. Grab any word the Lord gives you and run with it.

Holding crusades and preaching revival meetings is my dream and God-given assignment. What's yours? How many prophetic words will you receive about God's plans for your life before you get on the trail to make it happen?

Who told you that you're in a season of waiting? As members of the Body of Christ, we are in an era described in Amos 9:13 (KJV), *"Behold, the days come, saith the Lord, that the plowman shall overtake the reaper, and the treader of grapes him that soweth seed; and the mountains shall drop sweet wine, and all the hills shall melt."*

The Bible says in Isaiah 60:22 (KJV), *"A little one shall become a thousand, and a small one a strong nation: I the Lord will hasten it in his time."*

Stop leaving everything in the ethereal realm. You'll be seventy-one years old telling people, "I had a prophetic word over my life that God was going to use me to fill stadiums." Or "I was going to be one of the great businessmen of my day, and God was going to use me to fund His Kingdom in the last days." Nothing will ever happen if you leave it in the prophetic realm. You must take the words spoken by the Lord and do something with them. Move. Move now.

I was called into the ministry at eight years old. I was in Bible school by the time I was seventeen years old. If my parents would've let me, I'd have gone sooner. People talk about how they were called into the ministry at fifteen years old, but they still haven't started at fifty years old. Rest assured, God has probably called someone else by now.

Why haven't you done what God put on your heart to do? Why isn't it done yet? As a servant, the quicker and more accurately you carry out instructions, the sooner you get promoted. You become favored and treated as a choice servant.

 Get moving.

Faith without works is dead. I'm not saved by works, but I am expected to work to promote kingdom endeavors and build the Kingdom of God. I am the body of Christ on the Earth. The head wants to work through the body. Jesus is the head, and I'm a member of His body. I'm not just sitting around soaking in His presence. Our church has experienced rapid growth because we don't host soaking nights—we act. You don't have to choose one or the other, but actual soul-winning will outproduce praying for souls.

Starting a business or getting a job that produces income will outperform quoting scriptures on prosperity. Lend tangible action to your Christianity. That's what Jesus did. He laid his hands on the sick, gathered multitudes, and fed the hungry. I don't know who turned Christianity into a practice of talking about something that's coming. "There's going to be a revival coming. I see churches being built." Then build one! Get moving.

CHAPTER TWO

SEASONS OF WAITING ARE NOT SCRIPTURAL

When you encourage action instead of waiting, people often respond the same way they do when you talk about healing. They'll cite their five favorite scriptures that the Devil twists to keep them from getting healed. People love highlighting Job's struggle or Paul's thorn in the flesh. Meanwhile, the Bible is loaded with healing scriptures.

Likewise, people seem to have their favorite scriptures to support their excuse for inaction and remaining in a season of waiting. "The Bible says God had to take Moses to the back of the desert before He could use him." Let's address that one right now, and then I'll tackle the rest.

MOSES

Those who argue in favor of seasons of waiting say, "How many know God had to put Moses in the backside of the desert to shape him for forty years before he could lead Israel out?" God didn't send Moses out into the desert to train him. Moses's uncontrolled temper caused him to flee from a murder charge. He beat a man to death and buried him in the sand. That's a serious anger problem. If you get so angry that you black out and wake up covered in blood, having killed someone with your bare hands, you need therapy. In Moses's case, God provided him with forty years of it. It took Moses forty years to learn to control his temper—to crucify his flesh. Don't be like Moses in this area. His uncontrolled temper is what prevented him from entering the Promised Land. You, too, will need a season of waiting if you refuse to crucify your flesh.

Later, Moses's same uncontrolled temper caused him to hit the rock when God said, "Speak to the rock." Moses was angry; he disobeyed God in his anger, and it kept him from entering the Promised Land. He never fully gained control over his anger. When you're over a hundred years old and still having fits of rage, you have a serious anger problem. Please refrain from using Moses as an excuse for why you're in a training season in the desert.

Don't focus on the negative aspects of Moses' story and turn it into a doctrine. Moses also went on to lead a nation. That's the part of his story people should emulate, not the area of Moses' character that prompted a rebuke from God.

In addition, we have the Holy Spirit living inside of us, whereas Moses didn't have that luxury. The Holy Spirit changes you upon redemption. Peter is a primary example of how the Holy Spirit will change you in an instant. Once he received the Holy Spirit, he went from denying Jesus to a young girl at a campfire to proclaiming the Gospel of Jesus Christ to thousands of men.

JOB

According to Bible scholars, Job's ordeal lasted less than two years.

Job 42:10 says, *"The Lord gave Job double everything that he lost."* He lived to enjoy his family for another 140 years with wealth. He was two covenants behind us. The cause of Job's trial is not allowed to happen to a Christian today because we have been redeemed.

Satan was able to access Job based on his justification. The Devil told God, *"If you let me touch him, I can get him to curse you"* (Job 1:11). Job was justified by his own righteousness. Our righteousness does not justify us; we're justified by our faith in Christ. The means Satan used to accuse and attack Job could never be used to attack you and me.

Don't tell me you've suffered like Job for two decades. Not only was Job's situation a small portion of an otherwise prosperous life, but your situation is far different than Job's. You have been redeemed by the blood of Jesus and made righteous. What happened to Job can't happen to you.

JESUS IN THE STORM

Have you ever heard this one? "How many know Jesus and the disciples went through a storm? Sometimes, we go through stormy seasons in life." Allow me to prove this trite, religious statement wrong as well.

Jesus and His disciples were never in a stormy season. A storm came and went in one night. Jesus wasn't on a boat in the middle of a storm for fourteen years trying to get to the other side of an ocean. A storm came, it was rebuked, and it was over. If you've been going through a storm for years, it's time to seek a new captain. You can sail out of a storm, and you can rebuke the storm. You don't have to turn a storm into a season.

PAUL IN PRISON

Paul's thorn in the flesh is next on the list of misunderstood Bible references. Most references to this story usually begin something like this: "How many know even in your season of imprisonment we can trust God, and late in the midnight hour, when you least expect it, God will break you out?"

When that message is preached, people stand to their feet, clapping and shouting. People love messages that absolve them of responsibility or action. Paul was released from prison late in the midnight hour because he was thrown in jail at about 11:15 PM. He barely had time to pray and sing praises before he was broken out. Paul referred to his time in prison as a *"momentary light affliction."*

Brother Jesse Duplantis said the Lord instructed him, "Tell my people you've taken momentary and light and turned it into lifelong hardship." Do problems come? Yes. But God has given you the authority to deal with them on the same day.

DAVID AND GOLIATH

Another silly interpretation I've heard involves David and Goliath. "How many know Goliath mocked God for forty days? Forty represents a cycle of completion."

Goliath wasn't taken out because a forty-day cycle was finished. He was taken out because a seventeen-year-old boy refused to listen to some overgrown clown talk about his God for one more hour. He decided to take his head off right away. That's what ended the ridicule.

Moses, Job, Jesus in the storm, Paul in prison, and David and Goliath are the five favorite Bible stories used to justify a season of waiting, dry seasons, and seasons of attack. All five problems ended because a man acted. It had nothing to do with God's timing. In the cases of David and Goliath, Jesus in the storm, and Paul's imprisonment, each event ended in one day. What Moses endured was the consequence of his flesh and his fault entirely, and Job's problem can never happen to a New Testament Christian. Decisions create seasons.

 You're in control of your seasons of life.

CHAPTER THREE

DECISIONS CREATE SEASONS

If I tolerated strife in my marriage and decided to divorce Adalis, that would create a season of financial lack and backward steps in our ministry. It would additionally lead to a loss of credibility.

Decisions create seasons. A decision to cheat on my wife would be a decision to create a season of economic hardship. The Devil doesn't create my seasons, and God doesn't create my seasons. My decisions create my seasons.

Paul's decision to pray and sing praises to God in prison is what broke him out. David's decision to attack Goliath ended his season of mediocrity. Jesus' decision to rebuke the wind and waves ended the storm. Jesus literally changed His season. By commanding the storm to cease, He changed the weather. Elijah literally dictated seasons when he said, "There will be no dew or rain until I give the word" (1 Kings 17:1).

When you flip the switch and realize that you're not being assigned random seasons by God, but rather, you dictate your seasons, your whole life will change for the better. Jesse Duplantis has never experienced a financial deficit in forty-eight years of ministry because he never believed for it.

Bad decisions produce bad results. The Bible doesn't teach that Christians should accept their lot in life. For hundreds of years, the government used the Church to keep its people content to remain in the same condition, accept higher taxes from the king, and live a life of poverty. The same is true today. Our American government tells its citizens that they should be content with the bare minimum and live a stagnant life while they ride around in private jets. Unfortunately for corrupt government leaders, that's not what the Bible teaches. The Bible teaches that sin is responsible for lack and poverty, but God pulls you out of the pit and sets your feet on the rock to stand.

Many ministers say things like, "When times are good and there's a lot of money, I want to save and prepare for the lean times when there's less money." Where's that in the Bible? The Bible says we can go from "glory to glory," "victory to victory," and "strength to strength." Why do people always quote that in church and then make allowance for ups and downs? Deuteronomy 28:13 says, *"You'll always be the head, you'll never be the tail. You'll always be on top, you will never be at the bottom."*

As God said to Joshua, "Do not be afraid." Fear paralyzes. Fear sounds like:

"It's not a good time to buy buildings right now."

"It's not a good time to hire right now."

"They're forecasting an economic recession."

I don't care what "they" say. I'm not experiencing a recession. I don't have a long enough life to have a recession. I have eighty or ninety years on this Earth. I don't have time to experience what the world experiences. It's why I refused to shut our ministry down during Covid. I don't have time to take a year off for a disease that God promised to protect me from. I refuse to take even a month off. I'm not closing. I'm not slowing down. I'm advancing. It's time to move.

If you don't like the season you're in, change it. Do you know that you can do that in life? I used to hate fall because it meant summer was over. I like summer. I realized I could change my season with one Southwest Airlines flight. When summer ends in your region, it doesn't have to end for you. You can fly to Palm Springs, California, or Scottsdale, Arizona where it's summer year-round. There are people in Arizona who miss having a true winter season. It's an easy fix—fly to Colorado. Anyone can get on a plane and enjoy whatever season they desire. Fall doesn't bother me anymore because I know I'm only one Southwest flight away from any season I want.

Let's transfer this thinking into the spirit realm. If you don't like your current spiritual season, change it.

> **If you don't like your current spiritual season, you can change it.**

Moving is sometimes part of the equation, but many people are unwilling to move geographically. The average person lives and dies within a fifty-mile radius of where they grew up.

I'm going to provide you with three scriptural examples of people who made decisions that changed their season.

JONATHAN

> "We will cross over and let them see us. If they say to us, 'Stay where you are or we'll kill you,' then we will stop and not go up to them. But if they say, 'Come on up and fight,' then we will go up. That will be the Lord's sign that he will help us defeat them."
> When the Philistines saw them coming, they shouted, "Look! The Hebrews are crawling out of their holes!" Then the men from the outpost shouted to Jonathan, "Come on up here, and we'll teach you a lesson!"

"Come on, climb right behind me," Jonathan said to his armor bearer, "for the Lord will help us defeat them!"

— 1 SAMUEL 14:8-12

 The Lord will help you defeat your enemies and advance.

So they climbed up using both hands and feet, and the Philistines fell before Jonathan, and his armor bearer killed those who came behind them. They killed some twenty men in all, and their bodies were scattered over about half an acre.
Suddenly, panic broke out in the Philistine army, both in the camp and in the field, including even the outposts and raiding parties. And just then an earthquake struck, and everyone was terrified.

— 1 SAMUEL 14:13-15

When the Philistines had God's people pinned down, Saul instructed everyone to fast, and nothing happened. Jonathan refused to fast but instead chose to move forward and attack, and God gave him the victory. I'm not against fasting, but the man of action will always outperform the man who relies solely on prayer and fasting.

DAVID

...and had taken captive the women and those who were there, from small to great; they did not kill anyone, but carried them away and went their way. So David and his men came to the city, and there it was, burned with fire; and their wives, their sons, and their daughters had been taken captive. Then David and the people who were with him lifted up their voices and wept, until they had no more power to weep. And David's two wives, Ahinoam the Jezreelitess, and Abigail the widow of Nabal the Carmelite, had been taken captive. Now David was greatly distressed, for the people spoke of stoning him, because the soul of all the people was grieved, every man for his sons and his daughters. But David strengthened himself in the Lord his God.

Then David said to Abiathar the priest, Ahimelech's son, "Please bring the ephod here to me." And Abiathar brought the ephod to David. So David inquired of the Lord, saying, "Shall I pursue this troop? Shall I overtake them?"

And He answered him, "Pursue, for you shall surely
overtake them and without fail recover all."

—1 SAMUEL 30:2-8 (NKJV)

David did just as God instructed—He took action. He went after his enemies and retrieved everything that was lost. He changed his season. It was an unfortunate situation. His life was threatened, and he lost his wives and children. He encouraged himself in the Lord and asked God to help him get back what he had lost. God responded by telling him to pursue his enemies. He guaranteed David the victory and ensured that he would recover everything.

GOD IMMOBILIZED DAVID'S ENEMY

> When the Philistines heard that David had been anointed king of Israel, they mobilized all their forces to capture him. But David was told they were coming, so he went into the stronghold. The Philistines arrived and spread out across the valley of Rephaim. So David asked the Lord, "Should I go out to fight the Philistines? Will you hand them over to me?"
> The Lord replied to David, "Yes, go ahead. I will certainly hand them over to you."
> So David went to Baal-Perazim and defeated the Philistines there. "The Lord did it!" David

exclaimed. "He burst through my enemies like a raging flood!" So he named that place Baal-Perazim (which means "the Lord who bursts through"). The Philistines had abandoned their idols there, so David and his men confiscated them.

— 2 SAMUEL 5:17-21

The rock David launched at Goliath hit him on the forehead. It's not too often you see a baseball player get hit in the forehead with a baseball. It's not likely because human reflex would cause anyone to turn their head when they see something coming. So, who held Goliath's head still? Who immobilized David's enemy? When you take your position or make your move, God immobilizes your enemy. It's teamwork.

> But you will not even need to fight. Take your positions; then stand still and watch the Lord's victory. He is with you, O people of Judah and Jerusalem. Do not be afraid or discouraged. Go out against them tomorrow, for the Lord is with you!"
>
> — 2 CHRONICLES 20:17

You don't have to fight, but you must take your position. There's always a position you must take. Even when God fought for Israel, they had to first take their position and sing praises.

Jesus took action against the wind and waves.

David took action against Goliath.

 There's always a position you must take.

PART II
DESTINY-CHANGING DECISIONS

CHAPTER FOUR

DON'T ALLOW WHAT YOU DON'T DESIRE

"*Whatever you allow on earth, I'll allow in heaven. Whatever you forbid on earth, I'll forbid in heaven*" (Matthew 18:18). Jesus found this important enough to say twice. Your life will not be determined by what God allows; your life will be determined by what you allow.

I don't allow sickness. I don't make room for it. I don't allow it in my conversations. Don't claim ownership of sickness and disease by saying things like, 'my cancer,' 'my kidney disease,' or 'my heart problem.' If you don't want it, don't call it yours. Jesus took it. He can have it. Don't claim it.

I don't allow strife in my marriage or division in my relationship with my daughter, and it's apparent in my speech.

One time, I stopped at a gas station and bought several packages of candy for my daughter, Camilla.

"Who's that for?" a stranger asked.

"It's for my daughter. She's a great kid," I responded.

"How old is she?"

"Nine."

"Well, wait 'til she's a teenager."

"No, no, thank you. She's a great kid now. She'll be a great teenager, too," I replied.

I'm not making an allowance for future problems in my belief. I'm not making allowance for financial hardship. I reject it. I don't permit it.

CHAPTER FIVE

DO WHAT SATAN HATES

Ask yourself this question: If I were the Devil, what would I do to me? Then, discern whether what's happening in your life is from God or the Devil.

If someone offended you at church and, as a result, you've stopped going, do you think God wanted that? Do you believe you are participating in God's will for your life by not going to church? Is it possible the Devil was able to stop you by sending one moron to say something to bruise your ego? Maybe someone on staff at your church was up all night with a newborn baby and said something they shouldn't have said. Now you're allowing the enemy to use that offense to take you out of God's will. Who do you think is behind your reason for offense? Whenever you see Satan doing something, do the opposite of what he wants done and do it twice.

When I first started in ministry as an evangelist, meeting opportunities were slow to come—one here and one there. Sometimes I'd have to wait four and a half weeks between invitations. I looked forward to every precious opportunity to preach. One time, a pastor called six days before my scheduled meeting and canceled. There are two ways I could have responded to that. I could have made tea, pulled a blanket over me, watched TV, and sulked, or I could have seen it for what it was—the Devil's attempt to discourage me. The very first time this happened, I realized the disappointment was not God trying to discourage me by saying, "No son, you're not ready yet. I have you in a season of waiting." It was the Devil blocking the advancement of my calling. Sulking and crying were out of the question. My life is not determined by what God allows; my life is determined by what I allow.

When someone canceled one of my meetings six days out, leaving me nowhere to preach, something rose in my spirit. I started believing for two more meetings. If the Devil took one, I decided I wanted two back. I began praying and expecting two meetings. Even though I had no tangible way to get them, that's exactly what happened.

That type of response sends a powerful message to the Devil. It lets him know that if he attempts an attack against my life, it's guaranteed to fail. Not only will it fail, but I will punish him for targeting me. I want you to get this mentality in your spirit.

Don't make allowance for stagnation, it's unscriptural. Make up your mind early in life. If you lose a job, don't walk around talking about how you lost your job. Get another one that pays more. I set my faith that way, and so should you. Show the Devil that you're the wrong target. Let him know that he shouldn't mess with you. Tell him to pick on someone who believes in seasons of waiting. Someone prepared to spend forty years in the desert. Let him know, 'You'll have a better time with some chump, Mr. Devil. You're not going to have a good time with me. You've made a mistake choosing me as a target because I'm not a waiter; I'm a fighter.'

CHAPTER SIX

DETERMINE TO BEAR FRUIT IN EVERY SEASON

I know this might be a difficult concept for some people, but if you bear fruit in every season, it means you can't have any dry seasons.

> Oh, the joys of those who do not
> follow the advice of the wicked,
> or stand around with sinners,
> or join in with mockers.
> But they delight in the law of the Lord,
> meditating on it day and night.
> They are like trees planted along the riverbank,
> bearing fruit each season.
> Their leaves never wither,
> and they prosper in all they do.
>
> — PSALM 1:1-3

You bear fruit in every season.

I don't have dry seasons. If I were a car salesman, whatever the dry season is for selling cars, it wouldn't be dry for me. If I were a mortgage broker, I wouldn't have slow times. As a real estate agent, I'd have the most sales in December when everyone else is slow. I have a scriptural right to expect the bearing of fruit in every season.

The world can be in a dry season. I live in the world, but I'm not of the world. The years during Covid were not a favorable time for growth in ministry. We grew anyway. You get what you preach, and you get what you believe. You'll receive what you confess. Our church never would have experienced accelerated growth if I sat around and complained, "Well, people aren't interested in church. We're actually in a post-Christian society. The day of people gathering in buildings is over. People watch online now." No. The Word says:

> In the last days, the mountain of the Lord's house
> will be the highest of all—
> the most important place on earth.
> It will be raised above the other hills,
> and people from all over the world will stream
>   there to worship.
> People from many nations will come and say,
> "Come, let us go up to the mountain of the Lord,
> to the house of Jacob's God.
> There he will teach us his ways,
> and we will walk in his paths."

> For the Lord's teaching will go out from Zion;
> his word will go out from Jerusalem.
>
> — ISAIAH 2:2-3

Do fruit trees need to be motivated to produce fruit? No, it's what they do. Does a rooster have to learn to crow? No, that's what he does. I am a fruitful branch on the vine, bearing fruit is what I do.

I don't want you to read this and say, "Jonathan is right. I'm going to try to be more fruitful." It's not about trying. All you need to do is clear out every thought, belief, and influence that opposes what the Word of God says about you. That's why many new believers outperform Christians who have been in church for thirty years. Someone recently born again hasn't been pumped full of wrong teaching. They haven't been trained to say life's hard and unfair and things never work out.

It's impossible to shut me down. The correct belief and confession will make it impossible to shut you down, too.

 Fruitfulness is not your ambition; it's your birthright.

A ninety-nine-year-old billionaire living in Pittsburgh has several major projects taking place in his company right now. He does cryotherapy three times a day. *"As a man thinketh in his heart, so is he."* If you expect your body to start falling apart in your fifties, it'll start doing so in your late forties. Don't make room for it. See yourself as fruitful and strong in old age. The Bible says so in Psalm 92:14: *"Even in old age, they'll remain vital and green and shall produce fruit."*

Our covenant fathers lived through severe famines. Isaac experienced a famine, as did Abraham, according to Genesis 26:1. Jacob lived through none. The Bible tells us he sent his sons to Egypt to buy food. That enabled Joseph, by the gifts of the Holy Ghost, to solve the world's hunger problem. Our covenant forefathers lived through times when the Earth was in severe famine—not just recession. It didn't hinder their growth. God didn't give them just enough power to keep their heads above water while others went under. He raised them up to dominate in times of famine.

> A severe famine now struck the land, as had happened before in Abraham's time.
>
> — GENESIS 26:1

I'm sharing this with you because Abraham's blessings are yours and mine. All those who put their faith in Christ are the true seed of Abraham (Galatians 3:29). Through the new birth, the same thing that caused them to dominate in famine is in us. Abraham's blessings belong to you.

Do you think the mind of Christ is incapable of out-thinking the World Economic Forum? Do you believe they are more intelligent than you? Maybe they're smarter than your unredeemed mind, but they're not more intelligent than the mind of Christ you possess. God's plan enables you to bear great fruit no matter what happens.

> When Isaac planted his crops that year, he harvested a hundred times more grain than he planted, for the Lord blessed him.
>
> — GENESIS 26:12

During a time of famine, Isaac planted. He acted. He wasn't focused on the conditions of the ground or worried about needing the seed he planted for food. Isaac moved with an expectation to produce, even in a famine.

> He became a very rich man, and his wealth continued to grow. He acquired so many flocks of sheep and goats, herds of cattle, and servants that the Philistines became jealous of him.
>
> — GENESIS 26:13-14

The blessing of God on your life should provoke others to want to follow your God.

> 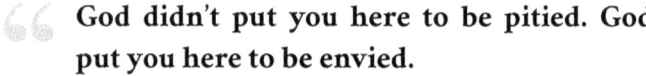 **God didn't put you here to be pitied. God put you here to be envied.**

CHAPTER SEVEN

REFUSE TO QUIT

J ust a few years ago, I couldn't afford a car. Now, not only have we bought buses to bring people to church by the hundreds, but I'm also traveling all over the country to preach in personal aircraft, and I don't even feel it financially. Don't worry about where you are now. Pay attention to where you're headed. *"Despise not the day of small beginnings, for your latter end shall greatly increase"* (Job 8:7).

> So the Philistines filled up all of Isaac's wells with dirt. These were the wells that had been dug by the servants of his father, Abraham.
> Finally, Abimelech ordered Isaac to leave the country. "Go somewhere else," he said, "for you have become too powerful for us."
>
> — GENESIS 26:15-16

Because Isaac was greatly blessed, the Philistines stole his land and deported him. When you advance, there will always be opposition. Supernatural advancement is your birthright. But when the Devil gets mad, and his people attempt to block your blessing, what do you do? You do what Isaac did.

> So Isaac moved away to the Gerar Valley, where he set up their tents and settled down. He reopened the wells his father had dug, which the Philistines had filled in after Abraham's death. Isaac also restored the names Abraham had given them.
>
> Isaac's servants also dug in the Gerar Valley and discovered a well of fresh water. But then the shepherds from Gerar came and claimed the spring. "This is our water," they said, and they argued over it with Isaac's herdsmen. So Isaac named the well Esek (which means "argument"). Isaac's men then dug another well, but again there was a dispute over it. So Isaac named it Sitnah (which means "hostility").
>
> — GENESIS 26:17-21

Isaac had three opportunities to quit, but he didn't. Isaac kept moving forward. I've heard many stories through the years of people who quit after experiencing setbacks. "Our ministry was doing very well, and then our accountant embezzled millions of dollars out of our ministry." People love to embrace a story that justifies why they're dry and not producing fruit.

I'm challenging you to make up your mind. Refuse to go to your grave with a story of why you never achieved greatness. The same thing that was in Isaac is in you through redemption. You're going forward, regardless of whatever injustices have been done. No one has the power to stop the Word of God that's been spoken over your life. You are like a tree planted by the water; in every season, you bear fruit. Your leaves never wither, whatever you do prospers, and nobody can stop that. The president can't stop it, and neither can 87,000 IRS agents. Whatever is being done to cause you to fear will not stop you.

Your forward motion is a decision. It's what God told Moses in Exodus 14:15, *"Stop crying out unto me. Tell the people to get moving!"* I'm telling you today, get moving. What is in your heart to do? Why haven't you done it yet? Why are you going to let today go by without having started it? Get moving. I didn't say, get it accomplished today. You'd have to have a pretty small dream for your life if you can get it done by bedtime.

> Abandoning that one, Isaac moved on and dug another well. This time there was no dispute over it, so Isaac named the place Rehoboth (which means "open space"), for he said, "At last the Lord has created enough space for us to prosper in this land."
>
> — GENESIS 26:22

The Devil is a quitter. Perseverance is a fruit of the Spirit, not a fruit of Hell. The Devil fought Isaac once. Then, he fought him a second time. After the third time, he decided to go pick on somebody who quits easier. He'd had enough of Isaac.

 If you don't give up, the Devil will give up.

Satan is a loser. He's a quitter. He tempted Jesus three times. Each time Jesus answered him out of the Word. After the third time, Satan left him alone. He didn't try a fourth time. If you don't give up, the Devil will find an easier target. Don't make yourself an easy target; make yourself a hard target.

They thought they could take Isaac's wealth. But they didn't understand it wasn't what they took that was blessed, it was Isaac who was blessed. People can attempt to take your stuff, but they can't take your blessing.

Our buildings are great, including our offices, studio, bible school, and church. A lot of money is wrapped up in these things, but that money came from the blessing of

God. It could burn to the ground. If it does, I'll build another one. *I'm* blessed. The only way the Devil can win is if he takes me out. But according to Psalm 91:11, he can't take me out either because *"He orders his angels to protect me wherever I go."*

CHAPTER EIGHT

FIND YOUR PLACE

God has a place for you to prosper. For Elijah, it was a brook called Kerith. For a widow, it was a place called Zarephath. For Peter, it was among the Jews. For Paul, it was among the Gentiles. God has a place with your name on it.

> Abandoning that one, Isaac moved on and dug another well. This time there was no dispute over it, so Isaac named the place Rehoboth (which means "open space"), for he said, "At last the Lord has created enough space for us to prosper in this land."
>
> — GENESIS 26:22

Life can't be filled with endless fighting. I wrote an entire book on spiritual warfare. I believe in it, but I believe in successful spiritual warfare. I don't believe in continual spiritual warfare. You shouldn't be engaged in a forty-year struggle. You should win and enter your Rehoboth. *"At last, God has given us space to prosper in the land."* God has a place with your name on it. He'll show you where to live. When He does, get there.

You're joined with Jesus, which means you are more than a conqueror. *"I can do all things through Christ who strengthens me"* (Philippians 4:13). You're not in a season of waiting. You're in a season of productivity, and that season will not end. What God gave Isaac through covenant, you have through a better covenant, built on better promises, in Jesus' name.

Get to where your blessing is and find your Rehoboth. Stop trying to make things work where you don't belong just because you grew up there. God has a Rehoboth especially for you. He hasn't forgotten about you. If this is the first time you've had someone tell you this, I'm happy to be the first to tell you: You're not in a season of waiting. You're in a season of supernatural acceleration. Time is short. Jesus is coming soon. It is time to find your place and get moving.

CHAPTER NINE

BEGIN TODAY

I want you to do two things before this day is over. First, I want you to take one step toward your destiny. That's a decision you can make.

What's the condition of your business's website? No excuses about a guy who said he would make you one for free, but he ended up not doing it, and you don't know how. Learn. Watch a YouTube tutorial. Get moving. Find the time to do what needs to be done.

What if you dropped all your laundry off at the cleaners and used the time you would have spent doing laundry to knock out that website? Would the effort result in more money than you paid the cleaners? You're worth more than you think. Sometimes, those closest to you are the slowest to see your worth, but you can decide to start proving it today.

Maybe you're someone who feels called to preach. Great. Stop *feeling* called to preach and start preaching. You don't need to schedule meetings. Go where there are people and start preaching. That's what Jesus did until the meetings opened up.

The second thing I want you to do is what Isaac did amid the famine: Sow a seed and mark it 'My dream seed.' Lack of resources deters many people from doing what God told them to do. In the natural, they're right. But you're not broke. You have a seed; you have something in your hand.

Elisha asked the widow, "What's in your house?" I'll ask the same to you. What do you have in your hand that can produce what your destiny requires and desires? What represents your best seed, a costly seed? What can you sow with your faith attached? As you sow, I'm believing with you. You will receive both the finances to fund your dream, and the favor to bring it to fruition. Favor will produce, in one day, the type of advancement that would take others twenty-five years. That's divine favor.

PART III
DESTINY-CHANGING ACTIONS

CHAPTER TEN

AVOID ZEAL KILLERS

This is a lesson from the life of Joseph. When God gives you a dream, there's zeal attached to it—an energy that comes with it. When you think about your dream, you get excited. If you want to know your purpose in life, consider what excites you. What excites you so much that you'd do it every day for free?

When Joseph shared his dream, his brothers tried to kill him. Not everyone is happy to hear about your future. Your family is least likely to see the greatness in you and the greatness of your dream. When David shared his plans for Goliath, he received no encouragement from his family—he received discouragement. An excellent way to make sure your dream is dead on arrival is to run it by people who are anointed by Hell to suck the strength out of you.

When it was time for our ministry to build a church building, I told very few people. If I were to share that openly, ninety-nine percent of people would say, "Well, I don't know if I'd do that now. Church attendance is down, building materials are at an all-time high, and we expect a recession." That's the response I would have received. I wouldn't have heard, "That's great. I'll give the first quarter million." Those people are rare.

CHAPTER ELEVEN

SEEK ACCOMPLISHED COUNSELORS

F rustration in life comes from having a destination without knowing how to get there.

> The labour of the foolish wearieth every one of them, because he knoweth not how to go to the city.
>
> — ECCLESIASTES 10:15 (KJV)

Pastor Rodney told me he saw a stadium full of people streaming toward the altar to get saved. How did I know how to get a stadium? How did I fill the stadium with people who needed to hear the Gospel? I spoke with people who have done those things before.

I once spoke with a married couple who run an awesome nonprofit. I had never heard of one like it before or since. The work they do is incredible. They wanted to do it full-time, but they didn't know how to make it profitable enough to make it their full-time employment. So, I put them in touch with someone who runs a similar non-profit. Instead of speaking to zeal killers about your dream, seek out those who have successfully done what you're trying to do.

Before buying land, I spoke with several people at length who understand real estate and land acquisition from a church perspective. That's what the Bible means when it says: *"In the multitude of counselors there is safety"* (Proverbs 11:14 KJV). Safety isn't found in stupid counselors but in good counselors.

Benson Idahosa had a saying, "Anyone who hasn't done the thing you're trying to do twice is disqualified from telling you how to do it once." If you're thinking about making a considerable land purchase, don't talk to people who don't own land. If you're considering building a home, don't discuss it with people who rent an apartment.

CHAPTER TWELVE

PRAISE

> And when they began to sing and to praise, the Lord set ambushments against the children of Ammon, Moab, and mount Seir, which were come against Judah; and they were smitten.
>
> — 2 CHRONICLES 20:22 (KJV)

The moment they began to give God praise, the Lord sent ambushments against their enemy. They started killing each other, dropped all their wealth, and fled.

Complaining magnifies trouble. Praise magnifies God. God will step into your praise and turn your season around immediately. When they shouted at the walls of Jericho, the walls didn't fall over time; they fell flat immediately.

Lift your hands now and say, "Father, I praise You for supernatural advancement."

CHAPTER THIRTEEN

ENACT THE POWER OF PRAYER AND FASTING

Job didn't randomly snap out of his troubles. He acted by praying for his friends. When he did, the Lord ended his captivity and restored double everything that had been taken.

> And the Lord turned the captivity of Job, when he prayed for his friends: also the Lord gave Job twice as much as he had before.
>
> — JOB 42:10

Prayer and fasting will change your season, as it did for Daniel. In Jeremiah chapter 25, he prophesied the Israelites would be in captivity for seventy years because they disobeyed God. When those seventy years came and went and the Israelites were still in captivity, Daniel fasted and prayed for an answer. The Lord sent Daniel's answer immediately. Prayer and fasting broke the Israelites out of Babylonian captivity (Daniel 9).

We begin every year with prayer and fasting; this year was no different. It's been an amazing year thus far. Amid recession, war, and chaos, we've supernaturally multiplied time after time.

CHAPTER FOURTEEN
CHANGE YOUR CONFESSION

Elijah changed seasons with his confession.

"There will be no dew or rain unless I give the word" (1 Kings 17:1).

"Today, I will call down fire from heaven, and we'll see whose God is stronger" (1 Kings 18:24).

"Get into your chariot, for I hear the sound of an abundance of rain" (1 Kings 18:41). At the time Elijah's servant reported there wasn't a single cloud in the sky.

Change your confession. Never use your mouth to amplify your enemy or your challenge. Use your mouth to change your seasons. Say this:

"I will pursue, I will overtake. I will recover all."

"If God is for me, who can be against me?"

"I have plenty of provisions."

"The windows of Heaven are open over my life and my business."

"I can do all things through Christ who strengthens me."

"I will prosper in the midst of famine."

Talk like that.

Kenneth Hagin said most Christians' trouble is "tongue trouble." Stop giving life to your storms. Stop giving life to your dry season. Your seasons are dry because you say they are. "I'm in a dry season." Keep talking like that, and you always will be. It won't even require any help from the Devil.

Start flipping it around by saying, "I'm not in a dry season. *I'm the head and not the tail. Always above, never beneath. Blessed in the city, blessed in the field. Blessed when I come in, blessed when I go out*" (Deuteronomy 28:1-14). That's what the Bible says. It's not just positive thinking. It's the covenant Word of God.

CHAPTER FIFTEEN

RUN WITH RUNNERS – DON'T SIT WITH SITTERS

Be a Jonathan, not a Saul. Saul sat, fasted, and starved. There's a time to pray, and there's a time to fight. When it's time to fight, it's a sin to pray instead.

John G. Lake said, "Oftentimes, men use prayer as a refuge to dodge the action of faith."

Run with the runners. Get around people who are doing something in life. Those who have moved to attend Revival Today Church have received a huge advantage. They get to be around people who are moving forward in life. It makes a difference. Your life will change when you make friends with people who are moving forward in life. Don't waste your time with a bunch of half-backslidden people, whose financial strategy is to have another baby to increase their welfare check. You won't find those types of people at our church. Instead, you'll see people come out of lack and oppression and move forward.

CHAPTER SIXTEEN

ENCOUNTER JESUS

There is someone you need to encounter; His name is Jesus Christ. In John chapter five, there was a man who was crippled for thirty-eight years. When he came in contact with Jesus, he began to walk. Thirty-eight years of stagnation was broken with one conversation with Jesus.

Meet Jesus. Get born again. Repent from sin. If you're living with somebody you're not married to, get the relationship under the blood in the marriage covenant or end it. Don't live with it. The man I referenced in John chapter five, whom Jesus made to walk again was told, *"Now you are better, so stop sinning, lest the worst thing come upon you"* (John 5:14).

You can't access the supernatural blessings I've referenced if you aren't in covenant with God. The only way to be in covenant with Him is through the shed blood of His Son, Jesus Christ.

The woman with the issue of blood spent everything she had on doctors and was no better—she was worse. But when she heard about Jesus and pressed in and touched Him, twelve years of struggle ended.

Jesus is a season changer. He empowers you to be more than a conqueror. Do you know Him? Are you living for Him? You can't half live for Him. Jesus will either be everything, or He'll be nothing at all. Jesus Himself said,

"Sell everything you have and come follow me" (Matthew 19:21).

"I have to bury my father first. He just died" (Matthew 8:21).

"Let the dead bury their dead." (Matthew 8:22).

Jesus' responses always insisted on either dropping everything and coming with Him, or staying where you are and forgetting it altogether.

AFTERWORD

Your decisions will determine your destiny, and no decision is more crucial to your destiny than deciding to have a relationship with Jesus. I challenge you to receive Jesus today. Maybe you've fallen away from Him and become an apathetic American Christian. Perhaps you found this book, or someone gave it to you, and you don't really know Christ. I want you to pray with me right now; He's one prayer away, one conversation away.

Pray this out loud from your heart:

> Heavenly Father, I admit that I've sinned. I repent. I believe in my heart that You raised Jesus from the dead. I confess with my mouth that Jesus is my Lord and my Savior. Right now, I receive forgiveness. By the blood of Jesus, I am saved. In Jesus' name, Amen.

If you prayed that prayer with me, I'd like you to visit www.revivaltoday.com/i-just-got-saved. When you fill out the form, I'll send you a Bible and other materials to help you live the Christian life.

The God of Breakthrough didn't show Himself to those who weren't doing anything. He showed himself to David, who prayed.

"Should I go?"

God replied, *"Yes, you should go. I'll deliver your enemy into your hand"* (1 Samuel 30:8).

David went, and he experienced the God of Breakthrough. You can experience the same breakthrough as David. I want that for you today, but it's up to you to decide. You must make a move.

If, after reading this book, you decide to make a change, I want to pray for you. Father, thank You for being the God of breakthrough. You have never changed, and You never will. I pray God will show you a way forward, today. I pray whatever God has stirred in your heart, He will give you the strength to do. I pray if anyone has stolen your zeal, it would be restored to you. May God give you a fresh zeal in Jesus' mighty name. May you have a great testimony of breakthrough and victory in Jesus' name, Amen.

If you decide to make a change in your life, it's essential to tell others. The Revival Today staff is available to talk and pray with you. Call the number below to speak to someone who cares about you and will pray with and for you. It's the most important decision you will ever make!

CALL 412-787-2578

"My generation shall be saved!"

— JONATHAN SHUTTLESWORTH

ABOUT THE AUTHOR

Evangelist and Pastor, Jonathan Shuttlesworth, is the founder of Revival Today and Pastor of Revival Today Church, ministries dedicated to reaching lost and hurting people with The Gospel of Jesus Christ.

In fulfilling his calling, Jonathan Shuttlesworth has conducted meetings and open-air crusades throughout North America, India, the Caribbean, and Central and South Africa.

Revival Today Church was launched in 2022 as a soul-winning, Holy Spirit-honoring church that is unapologetic about believing the Bible to bless families and nations.

Each day, thousands of lives around the world are impacted through Revival Today Broadcasting and Revival Today Church, with locations in Pittsburgh, Pennsylvania; Fort Worth, TX; Los Angeles, CA; and Phoenix, AZ.

While methods may change, Revival Today's heartbeat remains for the lost, providing biblical teaching on faith, healing, prosperity, freedom from sin, and living a victorious life.

If you need help or would like to partner with Revival Today to see this generation and nation transformed through The Gospel, follow these links…

www.RevivalToday.com
www.RevivalTodayChurch.com

Get access to our 24/7 network Revival Today Global Broadcast. Download the Revival Today app in your Apple App Store or Google Play Store. Watch live on Apple TV, Roku, Amazon Fire TV, and Android TV.

Call: 412-787-2578

- facebook.com/revivaltoday
- x.com/jdshuttlesworth
- instagram.com/jdshuttlesworth
- youtube.com/@jonathanshuttlesworth

DO SOMETHING TODAY THAT WILL CHANGE YOUR LIFE FOREVER

THUS SAITH THE LORD, **MAKE THIS VALLEY FULL OF DITCHES**. FOR THUS SAITH THE LORD, YE SHALL NOT SEE WIND, NEITHER SHALL YE SEE RAIN; YET THAT VALLEY SHALL BE FILLED WITH WATER... **THIS IS BUT A LIGHT THING IN THE SIGHT OF THE LORD**... AND IT CAME TO PASS... **THE COUNTRY WAS FILLED WITH WATER.**

2 KINGS 3:16-18; 20

Revival is the only answer to the problems of this country - nothing more, nothing less, nothing else.

Thank you for standing with me as a partner with Revival Today. We must see this nation shaken by the power of God.

You cannot ask God to bless you first, prior to giving. God asks you to step out first in your giving - and then He makes it rain. We are believing God for 1,000 people to partner with us monthly at $84. Something everyone can do, but a significant seed that will connect you to the rainmaker.

IF YOU HAVE NOT YET PARTNERED WITH REVIVAL TODAY, JOIN US TODAY!

This year is not your year to dig small ditches. When I grew tired of small meetings and altar calls, I moved forward in faith and God responded. God is the rainmaker, but you must give Him something to fill. It's time for you to move forward! **Will you stand with me today to see the nations of the world shaken by the power of God?**

Revivaltoday.com/give

revivaltoday.com/paypal

Zelle® info@revivaltoday.com

 @RTgive

Text "GIVE" to 75767
Call at (412) 787-2578

Mail a check to:

Revival Today P.O. BOX 7
PROSPERITY PA 15329

REVIVAL TODAY   Email: info@revivaltoday.com

www.ingramcontent.com/pod-product-compliance
Lightning Source LLC
Chambersburg PA
CBHW050034090426
42735CB00022B/3476